WOMEN'S RIGHTS IN THE WORKPLACE

A GUIDE TO PREGNANCY DISCRIMINATION

Jack Tuckner, Esq.

Copyright © 2013 Jack Tuckner, Esq.
All rights reserved.
ISBN: 1491264497
ISBN 13: 9781491264492
Library of Congress Control Number: 2013914619
CreateSpace Independent Publishing Platform
North Charleston, South Carolina

CONTENTS

CONTENTS

PREFACE

Why Women's Rights in the Workplace?

I've always been disturbed by all the injustice in the world, and the issues of women's oppression were right in front of my nose, but I couldn't see them clearly until 1991.

Back in the late 1980s—the crack years—arrests in New York City skyrocketed, and there was an urgent need for public defenders to represent the thousands of New Yorkers arrested on drug charges (the vast majority being African American and Hispanic). I signed up to do just that, dodging bullets inside (and occasionally outside) the Bronx County Criminal Courthouse, giving working, poor New Yorkers accused of crimes a zealous and caring defense.

This was deeply gratifying work, and I felt I saved the lives of more than a few in the process. I learned how to try cases to a jury, trying many and winning most of them too. But the criminal justice system is two-tiered, and on the bottom tier where most people are prosecuted, the system is corrupt and racist. The outrageous Rockefeller drug laws of the time required hellishly long prison sentences for relatively minor, nonviolent drug possession or sale charges. After a while, I was worn down by seeing the dissolution of so many people, so many kids' lives and families needlessly destroyed.

By 1991, I was trained, battle-tested, and looking to make a difference. At that very time, sex discrimination burst onto the scene through the first televised confirmation hearings of a US Supreme Court Justice nominee, namely Clarence Thomas. After his nomination was announced, he was accused of sexual harassment by his former assistant, Anita Hill, who worked for him when he ran the Equal Employment Opportunity Commission, ironically the agency charged with enforcing federal sex discrimination laws. And Thomas was the Commissioner, in charge of the entire federal agency.

Americans were riveted to this real-life, he-said/she-said drama taking place in the US Senate and beamed into living rooms around the country, because it raised the serious, but rarely discussed issue of gender relations in the workplace (and by only slight extension for the open-minded among us, issues of gender pay disparity, pregnancy dis- crimination and "glass ceiling" concerns).

Suddenly, we were hearing statistics such as sexual harassment touches the lives of 40 to 60 percent of working women and similar proportions of female students in colleges and universities. We learned there was no real protection as a practical matter for women facing workplace discrimination. The Family and Medical Leave Act had not yet been enacted, so women frequently lost their jobs when they gave birth to their babies and needed time off from work for maternity leave.

And in the summer of 1991, that's when it struck me: women, as a sex, were the largest oppressed minority group on the planet. And here in the feminist US of A, on the cusp of the twenty-first century, already deep into third-wave feminist thought and action, women were still burdened with second-class citizenship, with criminal and civil laws informed by the tiresome customs and practices of white male privilege.

Can you imagine? Right in front of my big white male nose the entire time and I didn't even notice it. Women don't earn what they're worth. Our sisters and mothers get paid 30 percent less than the men across the aisle doing the same or comparable job; our girlfriends and our daughters get hit on day and night by their supervisors and managers; and our wives get fired when they take time off to have our babies—and there doesn't seem to be a whole lot that we can do about it.

American women retain the exclusive hold on the bearing of our nation's children, it's our kids and families we're talking about here—yet we barely pay lip service to the needs of pregnant women before, during, and after their pregnancies. Still today, in 2013, **the United States remains one of only three countries out of 178 nations in the world that does not offer paid maternity leave benefits.** If I was looking for some wrongs to right and injustices to fight, I needed to look no further than the American workplace.

So that's how I found my calling representing women in discrimination matters, and in some ways, it's just as challenging as it's ever been for women today given the economic instability of our present day largely de-regulated, "free trade" decimated and hyper-masculin-ized economy. Consider how displaced our priorities are by this comparison: The US Supreme Court recently ruled that **corporations are persons** entitled to free speech rights (free speech!) under the Constitution, yet **the Equal Rights Amendment,** affirming the equal application of the Constitution to all persons regardless of their sex, was writ-ten in 1923 is still not in the US Constitution. Ninety years. Corporations are people, women not so much.

Women should expect to work in an environment free from objectification, free from sexual harassment, free from sexism, and free from gender pay inequality. Every single pregnant woman with a job should have the security of three months of paid maternity leave, and the same or comparable position waiting for her when she's ready to return to work.

I will continue to fight for the needs of working women and families as long as I'm a lawyer because for me, no other cause could be more important than helping to raise the status of women through law, one client at a time.

—Jack Tuckner

INTRODUCTION

PREGNANCY DISCRIMINATION

Approximately two-thirds of women who gave birth last year were in the labor force and working while they were pregnant, and many of those jobs and careers will be adversely affected by this otherwise wonderful event. Sadly, your pregnancy is inconvenient and unprofitable for your company, and your maternity leave will cause resentment, and will cost it time, money, aggravation, and resentment.

Given that American corporations primarily exist to profit as much as possible, there's little flexibility surrounding—and little feminine energy informing—the process of accommodating the needs of pregnant women in the workplace.

Are we a family values culture? Sure, but only for our own families, it seems. The message from corporate America to female employees: Your pregnancy is your problem—you're on your own.

Save for the privileged few, for most families in these recessional times, a woman's income is no longer a luxury but a necessity. The ability to maintain employment be-fore, during, and after pregnancy has become es-sential for the vast majority of American women. Though pregnancy and child-care demands affect women in the workforce at all levels, for lower-wage working wom-en the needs and challenges are often the greatest.

Given corporate America's penchant for outsourcing and off-shoring, it's becoming so competitive and nasty in workplaces that **some American companies misrepresent the law regarding pregnancy leave rights to their female employees, forcing them into resigning their positions the moment their baby is born. Don't let this happen to you.**

Pregnancy discrimination is illegal in every state in the union, yet it is thriving in workplaces all across the country.

This guide is designed to help answer frequently asked questions regarding pregnancy and your workplace rights.

It is our hope and intention to arm you with information to help you begin to navigate a system that is all too often stacked against you.

This is not a complete resource nor should it replace legal advice from a qualified employment lawyer regarding the specifics of your particular situation.

CHAPTER 1

DEFINING PREGNANCY DISCRIMINATION

In every one of these United States except Montana (go figure), employees are employed completely **"at-will;"** that's at the will, or whim, of your company. This means you can be fired at any time, for any reason, or for no reason at all. **Any time, any reason, or no reason at all.**

Unless you're the rare individual who can command a binding employment contract, or you're in the dwindling ranks of people still covered by union contracts, **you can be fired at the drop of a hat for any old reason, and unlike the way it works on** *Boston Legal,* **there's typically nothing you can do about it in real life.**

You can work somewhere for thirty years, walk in one day, and be told out of the blue, "Pack up; you're history," and it's perfectly legal. With only a few exceptions, **employers are not obligated to provide any notice or reason for your firing, and they are definitely not obligated to provide you with a severance package.** Not one thin dime.

Employers can fire you because the bookkeeper's brother, Jimmy, needs a job, or because they don't like the side you part your hair on. Seriously. One federal investigator explained at a workplace rights seminar that someone named Joe once tried to file a charge of discrimination at the Equal Employment Opportunity Commission (EEOC) after he was fired. When asked what reason his employer gave for firing him, Joe said that his boss told him he had to let him go because he had dreamed that Joe was the second gunman who shot President John F. Kennedy in 1963. The punch line was that Joe couldn't file a claim of illegal termination even though he wasn't even born when Kennedy was assassinated, because it's perfectly legal to fire someone for a crazy reason, as long as it's not a crazy *illegal* reason.

> **It's perfectly legal to fire people for crazy reasons, as long as they're not crazy *illegal* reasons.**

People regularly call our Women's Rights in the Workplace law firm with tearful tales of workplace woes. "My employer says that I lied/stole/lost a file/yelled at a customer/didn't make quota/was late all the time/had a bad attitude, etc., but it's not true, it's all lies." And if they've been fired, they often feel wronged, harmed, and betrayed. Yet, under United States law, **it's not illegal for an employer to fire you for any of those reasons, and as indicated above, it does not matter if the reason for your firing is "fair," silly, or a crazy, bald-faced lie.**

The only limitation on employers is that they cannot fire you for specifically illegal reasons.

YOUR WORKPLACE CIVIL RIGHTS

In general, except for individual or collective union contracts that protect less than 7 (seven) percent of the private workforce, **the only laws that provide protection for employees are the various federal, state, and city antidiscrimination statutes.**

Antidiscrimination statutes are the laws that protect employees from being "harassed" or treated differently from their coworkers, if the reason for the differential treatment is based on a "**protected status,**" which is, generally, an aspect about you that you cannot change, such as your race, color, national origin, sex (including pregnancy), age, disability, national origin, and so on.

You can be legally fired or harassed at any time, even if you happen to be, for example, the only Hispanic, older, pregnant, or disabled person in the workplace. An employer cannot fire or harass you **just because** you are Hispanic, older, pregnant, or disabled, but he can certainly harass you **when** you are Hispanic, older, pregnant or disabled. This distinction is vitally significant and important to understand. The discrimination has to be due to or because of that protected aspect of your identity.

For example, if you're a pregnant bartender in a restaurant and you're fired for continually providing incorrect change to customers and your employers have written you up for your carelessness several times, they can probably safely fire you and not worry about being sued for pregnancy discrimination. **Why? Because they can fire you for nondiscriminatory reasons *when* you're pregnant, they just can't fire you *because* you're pregnant.**

On the other hand, if you're the same visibly pregnant bartender who is fired because your employer feels that your "appearance" is now negatively affecting business, that would be discriminatory and illegal based on your sex (and pregnancy), and a violation of your workplace civil rights.

TWO BASIC QUESTIONS

People call our office and tell us dreadful stories of how hostile and stressful their work environments are, with micro-managing, incompetent supervisors who nitpick and criticize everything they do. Or they feel they're being "set up" to be fired.

We ask these callers two basic questions:

First, is this supervisor treating everyone with the same scrutiny or hostility? If so—if he's an **"equal opportunity" jerk**—then that's not discrimination, and it's not illegal. But if the answer is no–if he's just a jerk toward you and he singles you out for this hostile treatment–then that leads to the **second important question, namely, why you?**

If the answer to the "why you" question is, "He singles me out and treats me badly because I'm pregnant," or because "I'm a person of color," or because "I'm disabled," or because "I'm fifty-seven years old," or because "I declined his invitation to dinner and a movie," then you've squarely entered the protected discrimination zone. Now you must carefully navigate these challenging workplace waters.

Here's some general information to help you optimally handle the key decisions of your employment challenge:

First, you must understand that there are no employment laws that protect you from a generally abusive employer, even though you may be experiencing great distress. There is no law that states your employer must like you, respect you, or treat you fairly, as there are no laws requiring "fairness" or even civility in the workplace. Your employer is permitted to be evil, nasty and unpleasant so long as he or they are *equal opportunity* evil, nasty and unpleasant, that is to say, it's not illegal if they are evil, nasty and unpleasant to everyone without regard to sex, race, age, color, etc.

It's all about **discrimination**, also known as **differential** or **disparate treatment**. Workplace anti-discrimination statutes are **civil rights laws**. You are alleging a violation of your civil rights when you have an employment discrimination claim, and if push ever comes to shove in a courtroom, the burden will be on you to prove it. So, document everything.

WHY IS THIS HAPPENING TO YOU?

If your employer is, in fact, singling you out and harassing you by degrading the terms or conditions of your employment, the question you need to ask yourself is **"Why?"** Why is this happening? What is it about you, specifically, that causes your employer to treat you in this way?

For example, let's say everything was going along fine at work for the last four years; you've had good evaluations, and you received raises and bonuses. Then, a new manager is assigned to your department, and from the start you don't get along with this person. This is where the rubber meets the road. You need to ask yourself what's really going on here and give yourself an honest answer.

Is it because you possess more experience than this new manager, who may feel threatened by your competence level and superior skill set? Do your working styles clash? Is this a new manager who is hoping he'll make people want to quit to clear the way for his own hand-picked team? Maybe you haven't a clue why he's so tough on you. All of these reasons may be "unfair" to you, but unfortunately, there's nothing illegal about them.

Your employer is permitted to dislike you for no good reason. And if the new manager wants to bring in her own people and the company allows her, then you're likely out of luck. **Remember, you work at the will—one could say the whim—of your employers, and they do not have to justify the employment decisions they make.**

On the other hand, that manager may decide to marginalize you now because you are pregnant. He's anticipating that you will soon be so tired and compromised by the demands of a newborn baby that you won't be able to perform to his expectations. In this case, he may be discriminating against you because of your sex (sometimes referred to as "gender" in state and local laws).

> **Seven years after the FMLA took effect, over 357,000 leave-takers were downgraded to a lower position at work after their leave (US Department of Labor).**

Perhaps your peers have all been receiving promotions, bonuses, and prime work assignments and you have not, and you strongly suspect it's because of your pregnancy. Or you feel you've lost your footing and status once you return to work after your maternity leave. Or maybe you feel you're being treated worse than others because you're black, or gay, or fifty-six years old; or because you're Lithuanian, or Muslim; or because you questioned why you're earning less than a male colleague with fewer qualifications than you. Or you're being punished because you declined your supervisor's dinner invitation.

If any of these scenarios are occurring, you may be suffering from illegal employment discrimination. Without some identified **"protected status"** or **"protected activity"** (filing a discrimination complaint or requesting and taking maternity leave) that's causing your workplace challenges, even if you can prove your boss is a big jerk who's subjecting you to unfair and hostile treatment, there's no law against that. **An employer is allowed to be unfair, hostile, difficult, profane, bossy and rude, if that's what he's like with most everyone.** Or, if he's not like that with most everyone but only nasty and difficult with you, but you don't know why he's only nasty and difficult with you, that's legal too, unfortunately.

But he cannot be nasty, difficult, and rude because you just told him that you're pregnant—or because you're about to go out on maternity leave—or because you just came back from maternity leave. And he cannot be nasty toward you because you declined his sexual advances, or because you're gay (at least under many state laws), or because you had a recent health issue and asked for a reasonable accommodation, or because of your age, color, religion, ethnicity, national original, disability, and so on. Get it?

CHAPTER 2

YES, IT'S DISCRIMINATION.
NOW WHAT DO I DO?

If you feel you are being treated differently because of your pregnancy, follow this self-empowering strategy to protect yourself:

> **Bureau of Labor Statistics figures indicate that fully 80 percent of all working women will become pregnant at some point in their working lives.**

First of all, don't quit. "Quit" is a bad *four-letter word* to employee rights lawyers, so don't say it. Ever. Never resign. This is the single most important piece of advice we can offer. All of your power and legal leverage is lost when you quit your job and walk away.

To re-coin an apt phrase, **quitting is like *throwing out the baby with the bath water*.** You may think you have reached the point where you cannot take it one more day, but **resist the impulse to quit, because if you do, it's generally 'game over' and good-bye Jane.** You can forget about legal action. And even worse, if you quit, you probably won't be eligible to collect unemployment insurance benefits without a big, difficult fight, so don't do it. Don't quit.

> **While the average woman earns less than the average man, there is also a wage gap between mothers and non-mothers. The "mother's wage penalty" is estimated at approximately 7 percent per child, and just under one-third of the gap is attributed to the consequences of taking leave to care for children. Because a significant portion of the gender wage gap between men and women is due to differences in the work histories of men and women, access to paid leave that would encourage men to take it would help to reduce the stigma around taking leave, and is an important component of reducing the gender wage gap (Center for American Progress.com, April 16, 2012).**

Next, formally notify your employer of your grievance. What does this mean? **Generally, there can be no civil rights violation until your employer is 'on notice' of your belief that you are being treated differently,** which is another way to say you are being discriminated against in the workplace. Once you've done so, under the law, employers then have an opportunity to look into your concerns so that they can fix anything they discover that requires "corrective" or "remedial" action. You are also protected from corporate backlash by the mere act of formally complaining, whether they actually help you or not, but more on that later.

Moms earn up to 14 percent less than women who don't have children, says a University of New Mexico study (2012, NPR.org).

And **DO NOT QUIT.** It bears repeating; it's that important.

A 2013 *Harvard Business Review* study showed that women who have children are judged less competent and are less likely to be hired or promoted.

CHAPTER 3

WHAT'S THE BEST WAY TO NOTIFY MY EMPLOYER?

Put it in writing. Forget about an informal, verbal complaint; that's often more dangerous than not complaining at all. Why?

Because verbal communications can be denied, misunderstood, or misremembered. And if you are complaining about the way you are being treated and signaling to your management team that you feel it is because of your sex, your pregnancy, or your maternity leave, the company may not have the same view of the problem as you do. You don't want to give your employer an opportunity to find fault with you in reaction to your complaint or protected announcement and then fire you, for example. **You need to protect yourself under the law by generating a *paper trail* of your own protected grievances.**

Formal notification is provable, actual notice to the company. Put your complaint in writing, and send the letter in a way that proof of delivery can be shown, either by certified mail, or by a courier service such as FedEx or UPS that provides "tracking" information. You want a signature confirming that your letter was received.

This formal letter of notification serves two purposes. First, it alerts the powers that be at your workplace to your situation with the hope that it will be properly handled. Second, the formal notification protects you from **retaliation** under the federal and state employment discrimination laws that protect you from illegal backlash.

Keep the letter concise—less than one page in length— and don't forget to send it in a verifiable manner so their receipt of it can be proven if necessary later on.

Email is generally not an optimal method of sending the initial complaint letter unless you are assured of obtaining a "read receipt" message from the recipient. Email is fine to use once the investigation into your claims has begun and you are meeting with management and/or human resource people, who are questioning you and keeping you informed of the investigation status. When this occurs, each time you have another conversation with someone in management, we recommend sending an email restating what was said during the meeting and what each person committed to doing before the next meeting occurs, etc.

TO WHOM DO I SEND THE NOTIFICATION?

In companies large enough to have human resource ("HR") departments, the complaint letter should be sent to the director or the vice president of HR. If there is no HR department, send it to the highest-ranking corporate officer or to the person in the company with the most authority.

If this high-ranking person also happens to be the perpetrator of the harassment or the discriminatory treatment, then send the letter to the next highest-ranking person in the company.

In the occasional awkward situations where the harasser or perpetrator of the discrimination is the sole company principal, or the HR director is under the control of the perpetrator and there is no one else to notify, the letter should be sent to him just the same, even if he is the harasser himself. And it should be sent for the same reasons: to provide "notice" of the wrongdoing so steps may be taken to correct the discriminatory treatment and to formally document your complaint to protect yourself in the event that you suffer some adverse employment action, such as a firing, later on.

WHAT SHOULD THE NOTIFICATION SAY?

Keep it simple. The body of a pregnancy discrimination complaint letter might look something like this:

By FedEx

David Smith

Director of Human Resources

Patriarch's Publishing, PC

Corporateville, USA

Dear Mr. Smith:

Unfortunately, after much thought, I have concluded that I am being treated differently at PP ever since I told Paul Patriarch that I'm pregnant.

I'm still deeply upset over the remarks he made, when he told me that the insurance plan for a pregnant employee is way too expensive for PP at this time and I'm "not worth it," because he was angry that I'll be out on maternity leave during the busy fall season. He told me that I don't qualify for the FMLA, so I will have to quit when I have my baby because I don't have enough accumulated sick days, and PP doesn't have a maternity leave policy.

I have been a loyal and valued employee for the eleven months that I've worked for PP. I have yet to call in sick, brought in more revenue in six months than my predecessor did in three years, and I have nurtured strong relationships with my colleagues and clients, as my first and only "exceeds expectations" evaluation notes.

This is why I am so distraught at this recent turn of events, especially as I never expected that the news of my pregnancy would cause such a severely negative and hostile change in the terms and conditions of my employment. It is obvious that Mr. Patriarch is taking my pregnancy personally, as he has been punishing me and creating a hostile work environment since I told him I was having a baby. Please contact me at your earliest convenience to discuss these serious workplace concerns. Thank you.

Sincerely, etc.

> **Keep the letter concise—less than one page in length—and don't forget to send it in a verifiable manner, so you can prove it was received.**

The letter should include specific comments that were said to you and/or specific instances of discriminatory treatment that have occurred.

Specifics lend greater credence to your assertion that you are being treated differently. General language such as "he's hostile toward me" or "he's harassing me" is more difficult to address and therefore harder to investigate or correct. And as I mentioned before, he's allowed to be hostile toward you and to harass you; he just can't harass you or be hostile toward you because you're pregnant, etc.

CHAPTER 4

PREGNANCY, THE SPECIAL PROTECTED STATUS

Even if you are working for the most wonderful and progressive company on the planet, you never know what will happen when your status changes to "pregnant," so it's recommended you take these precautionary measures.

Never tell coworkers about your pregnancy before you officially notify your employer.

When first notifying the employer of your pregnancy, do it in writing, even if it's just a friendly, chirpy email notification to announce the exciting news and to inquire about the company's maternity leave policy, which you'll want to know about anyway.

You should do this even if there is no hostility or concern with your company's reaction to your pregnancy, as it leaves a record date-stamping the pregnancy notification (paper trail), and your possession of it will protect you in the event that something goes wrong later (and things seem to go wrong with predictable frequency once women announce their pregnancies at work). Doing this creates a record showing that **your employers knew you were pregnant** before they placed you on a performance improvement plan, for example, or before they fired you or otherwise diminished a term or condition or benefit of your employment.

Motherhood Penalty?

A study by Stanford sociologist Shelley Correll found that employers perceived women with children to be less competent than their counterparts.

Women without children are eight times more likely than mothers to be recommended for management.

National Women's Law Center Vice President and General Counsel Emily Martin: "Pregnant workers are ready, willing, and able to continue working, but they are often forced out by employers who refuse to make minor accommodations. These women and their families pay a steep price when they're pushed out of jobs. There's no reason for pregnancy to be a job-buster."

By giving notice of your pregnancy in writing, you are protecting yourself in the event that conditions at your workplace change. For example, everything may have been going along swimmingly with your job, but you suddenly notice that you are not being fed the good sales leads because your manager feels you won't be there to follow up on them given your upcoming three-month maternity leave. That would be sex and pregnancy discrimination, which could have a significant impact on your performance review, your income, and your future.

If your fall from grace at work was occasioned by your pregnancy notification, that would be illegal discriminatory treatment, and then you would want to send the more formal complaint notification discussed above.

CHAPTER 5

I SENT MY LETTER. NOW WHAT DO I DO?

The short answer is **WAIT. And DON'T QUIT.**

There is nothing to do until you see how your employer responds to your complaint letter. It's a bit like a chess game. You need to see how they react or respond before you can know what move is best for you to make next.

Here's a brief list of things NOT to do...

1. **Don't quit.** You may be tempted and it might feel good in the moment, but your chances of receiving financial compensation for your claim are greatly reduced if you resign. You maintain your power and legal and economic leverage by maintaining your job. **Think: out of sight, out of mind.** And to add insult to this self-inflicted injury, if you quit, you won't even be eligible to collect unemployment insurance benefits.

   You wrote a letter of complaint to the company primarily because **the law requires you to give your employer a reasonable opportunity to address your allegation of discriminatory**

23

treatment. The company is allowed the opportunity to correct its mistakes. Secondarily, **you are standing up for yourself by drawing a line in the sand and declaring that it's not OK for them to treat you this way.** You expect them to hear what you're saying, investigate your complaint, and take whatever action is necessary to correct the current discriminatory treatment and injustice. If your employer takes your complaint seriously and takes positive action in response, that's wonderful, as you've shown optimal regard for yourself, and you were heard and acknowledged and the matter was addressed.

On the other hand, if they treat you even worse after you complain (or after you notify them of your pregnancy), **the fact that you have a complaint on record will go a long way toward solidifying your "case" of discrimination (and/ or retaliation).**

When companies take meaningful corrective action to address a protected complaint, they have met their legal obligation. You are generally not entitled to a monetary settlement for the stress and aggravation the discrimination may have initially caused you before you complained.

Remember, you can always be fired *when* you're pregnant; you just can't be fired *because* you're pregnant.

This would mean you'll have more leverage to negotiate an appropriate settlement or severance package, and in the unlikely event that you do wind up in court later on, your original complaint letter that was provably filed with your company can mean the difference between winning and losing your discrimination lawsuit.

2. **Don't file a complaint with a governmental agency until you understand your options.** Often, in the heat of the moment and wanting to take some tangible action, people will run to file a claim with a federal or state administrative agency (such as the US Equal Employment Opportunity Commission). This can be a mistake, as there are a number of factors to con-sider when deciding where, when, and even if a complaint of discrimination should be filed at any given point. Filing with the wrong agency (or court) or filing at the wrong time can greatly limit your options and ultimate outcome. Check with an experienced employment lawyer before committing to an actual complaint filing, whether administrative or judicial. Filing a complaint should be your last step, not your first.

3. **Don't do anything that might put you at risk for being fired for cause.** This is very important. While you are in discussions with your employer regarding your workplace challenges, you'll

want to take the high road. **Don't do anything that will give them an excuse to fire you for insubordination, uncooperativeness, etc**.

You are still an employee and must follow the rules. If the rule is to be on time, then be on time. During the sensitive few days or weeks while they are investigating your complaint, strive to dot every i and cross every t. **Just because you've notified your employer of your pregnancy (or your discrimination complaint) doesn't protect you from being terminated. Remember, your employer can happily fire you when you're pregnant and not sweat it too much if they're confident that they have a strong non-discriminatory basis, so try not to give them any reason to question your solid performance or timeliness and attendance.**

4. **Consult with an experienced employment lawyer.** Each situation is unique, and there isn't a one-size-fits-all strategy. Before push truly comes to shove, you'd be wise to do some online research for yourself and consult with a qualified and experienced employee rights lawyer to determine your most optimal and empowering strategy.

5. **Don't quit.** Have you heard? All too often, people call us for guidance only *after* they've al-

ready resigned because they felt they couldn't stand it one second longer, only to discover that they've undermined their potential discrimination claim. **Get legal advice before you throw in the towel.**

CHAPTER 6

WHAT ARE MY MATERNITY LEAVE RIGHTS?

Are you entitled to maternity leave? Almost certainly yes, but size matters. The size of the company, that is.

There are two basic federal laws that protect pregnant employees from discriminatory treatment. The one most people know is the Family and Medical Leave Act of 1993.

The FMLA entitles eligible employees of **companies with fifty or more employees** to take **unpaid, job-protected leave** for specified family and/or medical reasons.

To be eligible under the FMLA, at the time of your baby's delivery, you must meet the following three criteria:

1. You must have worked for the company for the past twelve months.

2. You must have been working roughly full-time hours (1,250 total hours worked).

3. The company you work for must have at least fifty employees (within a 75-mile radius).

If you meet the eligibility requirements, you're entitled to take up to **twelve workweeks per year of unpaid maternity leave,** and you won't have to live in fear of being fired.

If you don't meet the above criteria, then you are not covered under the FMLA, and **you have no federally protected right to take a set amount of maternity leave.**

If your company has fewer than fifty employees or you have not worked for the company for at least one year, you may still be covered under the federal **Pregnancy Discrimination Act of 1978 ("PDA").**

The PDA is an amendment to the Civil Rights Act of 1964, and it prohibits sex discrimination on the basis of pregnancy in **companies with a minimum of fifteen employees.** So, if your employer has fifteen or more employees and you're informed that you will have to resign because you are not eligible for maternity leave, they are likely violating the law by discriminating against you "on the basis of pregnancy, childbirth, or related medical conditions," as well as on the basis of your sex, because **pregnancy is clearly a female sex-specific activity.**

This law states that your pregnancy may not be treated differently than your employer would treat any other person with a disability, temporary or otherwise. So, if your employer has made a "reasonable accommodation" to a coworker who broke her leg in four places skiing and was in traction for six weeks, or if other employees are permitted varying recovery times when they are sick with the flu, or recovering from a heart attack, or need eight weeks off for cancer treatment, your employer must similarly accommodate your recovery period following your baby's birth.

If they don't fire everyone else who becomes temporarily injured or ill and they allow them to return to work within a reasonable recovery period, they cannot treat your postpartum recovery any differently, and they would be required to hold your position open for a reasonable period following the birth of your baby. Generally, six to eight weeks is considered a reasonable convalescence following a vaginal delivery and eight to twelve weeks following a Cesarean section delivery.

States and Cities Provide Additional Protection

Most states and many cities have their own antidiscrimination laws that are often more comprehensive and progressive than federal law. In New York, for example, both the state and the City of New York have discrimination statutes that provide more protection to pregnant women than federal law provides. These statutes are more liberal in their definition of what constitutes a legally protected period of disability as it relates to pregnancy before and after your baby is born.

Also important to note is that in both the State and City of New York, for example, your employer need only have four employees on payroll to be covered under the pregnancy discrimination laws, as opposed to the fifteen employee threshold needed under federal law or the fifty people your company must employ before you qualify to take maternity leave under the FMLA.

So it's important to research your state and local employment discrimination laws, as it is likely that smaller companies with fewer than fifteen employees are covered under your state or city laws.

> **To see your rights by state, check this map:**
> **www.legalmomentum.org/**
> **Pregnancy_Laws_Map**

If you work for a small company in **New York** or **Connecticut**, for example, where the state laws require only four employees for coverage under workplace discrimination laws, your employer cannot treat your baby's birth any differently than they would treat an employee with a winter's bout of influenza, or with a heart attack that requires hospitalization and a two-month recovery period. **The employer must attempt to reasonably accommodate your disability to allow you to remain gainfully employed. Reasonable accommodation** involves a balancing act between the needs of the business and the needs of the temporarily disabled person. What's important here is that employers cannot exclude the postpartum disability known as, "I-just-had-a-baby-so-I-can't-come-to-work-for-a- while syndrome." **If they tell you** that you don't qualify for maternity leave because you're not covered by the FMLA (and some employers say just that), they're misrepresenting the truth and likely committing sex and disability discrimination.

CHAPTER 7

FMLA EXTRA: EMPLOYERS OFTEN MISREPRESENT MATERNITY LEAVE LAWS

In our women's rights employment law practice, I've noticed that when some companies take to advising their employees of their FMLA rights, they say that if all the criteria of the FMLA are not met—such as you haven't worked a full twelve months before your baby's birth or the company doesn't have fifty employees—then you're out of luck. They say that unless you have eight weeks of vacation time accrued, you'll have to resign. They tell you to look online so that you can see for yourself that you haven't met the requirements for an FMLA leave. But they don't bother to mention the **Pregnancy Discrimination Act** or the state and city laws that provide maternity leave protection. Remember, if you quit—even if they fool you into quitting–you **won't be eligible to collect unemployment insurance benefits.** So educate yourself through research and/or a consultation with an experienced employment lawyer in your region, and do it early enough in your pregnancy that you will know your rights when you speak with your employer.

(HAPTER 8

I AM BREAST-FEEDING MY BABY. AM I ALLOWED TO EXPRESS MILK DURING WORK?

Yes, if you work for a company with at least fifty employees. Signed into law in 2010, the Affordable Care Act amended Section 7 of the Fair Labor Standards Act to require "**reasonable break time for an employee to express breast milk for her nursing child for one year after the child's birth each time such employee has need to express the milk.**"

Employers must provide a private, intrusion-free, shielded-from-view area other than a bathroom. The length of time and number of breaks are subject to the needs of the nursing mother.

The employer does not have to compensate the employee for each of the breaks she takes for breastfeeding purposes. To be clear, if a nursing mother takes four fifteen-minute breaks each day, technically that's one hour of unpaid time.

Each state may have additional laws and provisions protecting nursing mothers. In New York State, for example, all employers, public and private and regardless of size, must accommodate the needs of a nursing woman to express breast milk for up to three years following the birth of her baby.

CHAPTER 9

REASONABLE ACCOMMODATION

The Pregnancy Discrimination Act (PDA) prohibits discrimination based on pregnancy when it comes to any aspect of employment, including hiring, firing, pay, job assignments, promotions, layoffs, training, fringe benefits such as leave and health insurance, and any other term or condition of employment.

> **More than 40 percent of full-time low-wage workers report that they're not allowed to decide when they take their breaks (NWLC Report, June 2013).**

If a woman is temporarily unable to perform her job due to a medical condition related to pregnancy or childbirth, **the employer must treat her in the same way as it treats any other temporarily disabled employee.** For example, the employer may have to provide light duty, alternative assignments, disability leave, or unpaid leave to pregnant employees if it does so for other temporarily disabled employees who are not pregnant.

> **This means a pregnant woman's manager can tell her when she can use the lavatory or have a drink of water.**

Also, some impairments resulting from pregnancy such as gestational diabetes or preeclampsia may be disabilities under the Americans with Disabilities Act (ADA). An employer may have to provide a reasonable accommodation (such as leave or modifications that enable an employee to perform her job) for a disability related to pregnancy, absent undue hardship (such as significant difficulty or expense). Some state and city antidiscrimination laws (such as New York's) provide even greater protection for working women experiencing pregnancy-related medical challenges.

> **• Today, nearly two-thirds of first-time mothers work while pregnant, compared to less than half in the 1960s (NWLC Report, June 2013).**

Even though the Civil Rights Act of 1964 prohibits discrimination based on sex, and the Pregnancy Discrimination Act prohibits workplace discrimination based on pregnancy and pregnancy-related disabilities, current employment laws are inadequate to protect pregnant workers on the job *before* their babies are born. Some federal courts have interpreted the existing laws as not requiring employers to make minor job modifications for pregnant women unless they have an actual pregnancy-related disability. So, for example, a pregnant cashier who asks for a stool to sit on for part of her workday may be forced to quit or to take an unpaid leave when her employer refuses to provide the stool.

While this is sex, gender and pregnancy discrimination in my view, and in the view of some state and city jurisdictions such as New York, under federal law it is arguably legal to refuse to provide the stool to that pregnant cashier, and the rationale for such stinginess is that the stool is required not because of her doctor's orders for a specific pregnancy-related condition, but simply because she's pregnant, and pregnancy is not a *per se* disability, so the employer can refuse the reasonable accommodation. Such a refusal may be nasty, shortsighted and bad for business, but it's technically not illegal.

That's why what's really needed now is the passage of the Pregnant Worker's Fairness Act, a bill **"to eliminate discrimination and promote women's health and economic security by ensuring reasonable workplace accommodations for workers whose ability to perform the functions of a job are limited by pregnancy, childbirth, or a related medical condition."**

Unfortunately, this bill was introduced and assigned to a congressional committee on May 14, 2013, where its chances of getting past the committee is 8%, and its chances of becoming federal law are 1%, according to the statisticians at www.gov.track.us.

Pregnant women, especially low-wage women in physically demanding jobs, frequently get pushed out of their jobs or must take unpaid leave when they request a modest, temporary accommodation, like a stool to sit on, more frequent restroom breaks, or temporary relief from heavy lifting.
(http://nywomensequality.org)

CHAPTER 10

NEXT STEPS—THE PREGNANT WORKERS FAIRNESS ACT—A VICTORY FOR NYC EMPLOYEES

As mentioned in Chapter 9, while employers usually understand that workers with limitations caused by disability have a legal right to reasonable accommodations, they sometimes view workers with limitations due to pregnancy as having no legal right to similar flexibility. While this law firm has successfully argued that such a distinction with a sexist difference amounts to illegal discrimination, the fact remains that some pregnant employees will lose their jobs when they ask for temporary modifications of their duties because of pregnancy, such as avoiding heavy lifting, or being permitted to sit down during a long shift, as these accommodations are needed not because of any particular disability, but merely because of the pregnancy itself, but pregnancy—in and of itself—is not a disability. That loophole in the PDA has permitted unscrupulous employers to deny some workers' requests, forcing pregnant women to quit, or to take unpaid leave, if they're not outright fired.

That's where the Pregnant Workers Fairness Act (PWFA) comes in. The PWFA just became law in New York City in

43

September 2013, but the federal PWFA (H.R. 1975 and S. 942) was introduced in Congress in May 2013, where the bill is stalled in the worker-unfriendly House of Representatives, so there's little hope it will pass any time soon.

But let's celebrate the victory for those who work in New York City, as the PWFA now requires that employers in the five boroughs of NYC must provide reasonable accommodations to pregnant workers who need them (unless doing so would impose an undue hardship). If a pregnant cashier needs to use a stool occasionally during an 8-hour shift, now her employer must provide it; if a pregnant administrative assistant requires additional restroom breaks or water drinking breaks so she stays optimally hydrated, management must allow her to do so; and if a pregnant police officer needs a desk re-assignment for several months as she can no longer don her Kevlar vest over her expanding belly, her superior officers must allow that temporary reassignment.

Some of these accommodations may have been provided anyway based on arguments that failure to do so would amount to sex, gender, or pregnancy discrimination, not to mention immorality, but it's important to have a law on the books that specifically forces employers to do the right thing and provide specific protections for pregnant workers, especially low-wage workers, who are most likely to work physically demanding jobs, and whose workplaces are more likely to be less flexible in their policies.

HELPFUL RESOURCES FOR MORE INFORMATION

http://www.legalmomentum.org/Pregnancy_Laws_Map

The above link provides a state-by-state map showing pregnancy discrimination, leave, and breast-feeding laws.

http://www.nwlc.org/sites/default/files/pdfs/pregnant_workers.pdf

This is a recent report from the National Women's Law Center and A Better Balance entitled "It Shouldn't Be a Heavy Lift: Fair Treatment for Pregnant Workers."

http://www.eeoc.gov/laws/types/pregnancy.cfm

http://www1.eeoc.gov//eeoc/publications/fs-preg.cfm?renderforprint=1

These two links are to the US Equal Employment Opportunity Commission (EEOC) website page on federal pregnancy rights.

http://exchange.nela.org/findalawyer

This link is to the National Employment Lawyers Association, a good site to search for a qualified plaintiff's attorney to consult with for advice regarding your specific circumstances.

Or visit us at http://womensrightsny.com or call us at 212.766.9100 or 800.FEM.LAWS.

ABOUT JACK TUCKNER

Jack Tuckner is the co-founding partner of Tuckner, Sipser, Weinstock & Sipser, LLP, a New York City employment discrimination boutique, exclusively representing employees in a wide range of labor and employment matters in federal, state, and city administrative proceedings, as well as in state and federal courts. His firm is committed to the ongoing struggle for workplace equality, providing vital and ongoing advocacy for those who have been undermined and marginalized by unjust employment practices. The firm concentrates its practice in the representation of women facing gender inequality in the workplace with respect to compensation, sexual harassment and pregnancy discrimination, as well as all other forms of illegal workplace discriminatory and/or retaliatory treatment.

**For more information, please visit us at
www. womensrightsny.com.**